DATE DUE

BODIES IN

CRISIS

ENVIRONMENTAL

D I S E A S E S

Jon Zonderman and Laurel Shader, M.D.

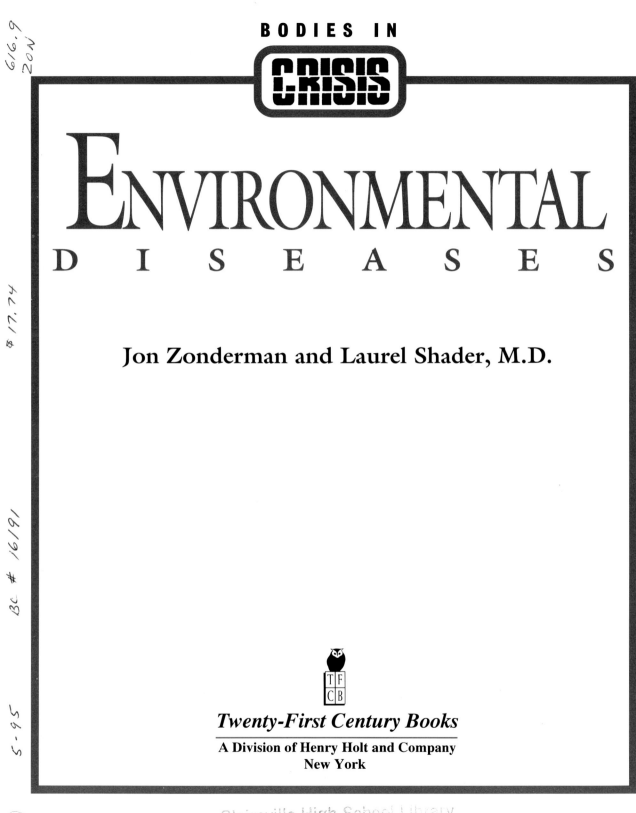

Twenty-First Century Books

A Division of Henry Holt and Company
New York

Twenty-First Century Books
A Division of Henry Holt and Company, Inc.
115 West 18th Street
New York, New York 10011

Henry Holt® and colophon are trademarks of Henry Holt and Company, Inc.
Publishers since 1866

Published in Canada by Fitzhenry & Whiteside Ltd.
195 Allstate Parkway, Markham, Ontario L3R 4T8

Printed in Mexico
All first editions are printed on acid-free paper ∞.

Created and produced in association with Blackbirch Graphics, Inc.

Library of Congress Cataloging-in-Publication Data

Zonderman, Jon.
    Environmental diseases / Jon Zonderman and Laurel Shader, M.D. — 1st. ed.
       p.   cm. — (Bodies in crisis)
    Includes bibliographical references and index.
    Summary: Discusses current studies on the influence of environmental factors on health and disease.
    ISBN 0-8050-2600-2 (acid-free paper)
    1. Environmentally induced diseases—Juvenile literature. [1. Environmentally induced diseases. 2. Diseases.] I. Shader, Laurel. II. Title. III. Series.
    RB152.Z65 1993
    616.9'8—dc20
                                         93-25911
                                            CIP
                                            AC

Contents

Exposing yourself to the natural elements can cause potential risks to health. Too much direct sunlight, for example, can cause a number of skin problems including burns, rashes, and even cancer.

1

The World Around Us

The world can be a dangerous place.

Our natural environment can be the source of a number of acute illnesses and long-term chronic diseases. Many people are allergic to insect bites and stings. Plants such as poison ivy, oak, and sumac can cause terrible skin rashes. And the sun probably causes more kinds of cancers—some easily treated and others very dangerous—than any other environmental factor. There are also a number of naturally occurring bacteria and parasites present in water that can cause illness and even death.

And when humans begin changing the natural environment—either the "micro" environment in which an individual lives and works or the "macro" environment in which we all live and work—there is an even greater risk of potential illness and disease.

When the early humans first abandoned their no-madic existence thousands of years ago and began settling in villages, they realized that many people were becoming ill from the human and animal feces that collected near their homes. The solution was moving the animals away from the houses and creating bath-room facilities away from dwellings for people to use.

Later, the first public sanitation systems were cre-ated. Using gravity and ground water, open sewers were dug and people emptied their household waste into a running system. But when heavy rains and flooding came, the sewers overflowed all through the villages. This led to outbreaks of life-threatening bacterial dis-eases such as cholera and typhoid fever. These diseases are still common in some third-world countries.

In industrialized nations today, disposal of house-hold waste is accomplished either through individual home septic systems or through public sewer systems. Both hold wastewater in a tank, where natural bacteria break down the waste components over time.

Although we don't know if prehistoric peoples de-veloped occupational illnesses (illnesses caused by a person's work environment) from the dust created by chipping stone tools or filing metal tools, we do know that in the Middle Ages the dangers of lead and mercury were recognized. The expression "mad as a hatter," came about because people recognized that many hatmakers seemed to be mentally unbalanced. Today we know that long-time exposure to the mercury used by hatmakers can cause brain damage.

A pioneer woman
empties a bucket of
wastewater near her
well. Many years ago
in America, diseases
were commonly
transmitted through
water contaminated
by sewage and other
wastes.

Harmful air pollution in our environment is caused by a number of factors, including buses and many other vehicles used for transportation.

Pollution

"Pollution" comes in many different shapes and sizes. And those who cause pollution are not simply "bad" people with no concern for the environment in which they live. In fact, each of us causes some pollution in our day-to-day living, and we all use or consume things

that create pollution as a by-product of their manufacture. Here are some examples:

• Many of the chemicals used to grow most of the food we eat—fertilizers, herbicides, and pesticides—cause pollution. Few people eat a diet of foods grown organically (totally without chemicals).

• Every manufacturing process consumes some natural resources and creates some waste, which becomes pollution as it is disposed of in the environment.

• Transportation by car, bus, boat, plane, or train consumes fuel that causes pollution when it is refined. Even more pollution is emitted from vehicles as the fuel is burned.

To be sure, in the highly industrialized parts of the Americas, Europe, Asia, and Australia, the population is growing increasingly aware of the need to try to control the unavoidable sources of pollution. But vast parts of Asia and almost all of Africa create massive amounts of waste, without sophisticated antipollution strategies at either the factory or community level. Yet even the best pollution-control systems do not completely do away with the problem. To a large extent, pollution in a modern society cannot be avoided.

New Problems, Old Problems

As we continue to change our environment, we open up the possibility of causing new illnesses and diseases. Even as we clean up many of the dangers created by previous generations of polluters, we face new threats every day.

We continue to send rockets into space, while we work to clean up toxic waste dumps. Many of these rockets not only leave spent fuel in the upper atmosphere, but also nuclear-powered engines circling the globe. As we encourage farmers to use less pesticides, herbicides, and chemical fertilizers in agricultural production, we as a society are encouraging the genetic altering of fruits and vegetables without fully knowing the consequences this will cause a generation or two from now. Similarly, use of growth hormones to encourage production of more milk in cows is quite common. Our increasing levels of knowledge and technology may have negative side effects in the future.

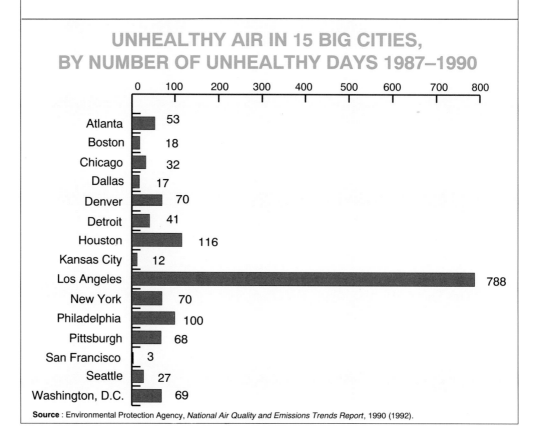

UNHEALTHY AIR IN 15 BIG CITIES, BY NUMBER OF UNHEALTHY DAYS 1987–1990

City	Days
Atlanta	53
Boston	18
Chicago	32
Dallas	17
Denver	70
Detroit	41
Houston	116
Kansas City	12
Los Angeles	788
New York	70
Philadelphia	100
Pittsburgh	68
San Francisco	3
Seattle	27
Washington, D.C.	69

Source : Environmental Protection Agency, *National Air Quality and Emissions Trends Report*, 1990 (1992).

Weighing the Risks

While we know about chemical pollution, we are still not sure whether electromagnetic fields from power lines and even from household items like microwave ovens and computers cause illness or long-term disease.

All this is not to say that progress is necessarily bad, or that we need to strive for a pollution-free world— which is technically impossible. What we do need to do is weigh the risk of environmental illness or disease with the benefits we enjoy in a modern world.

We also need to weigh the risk of environmental disease in relation to other risks we encounter daily. The number of illnesses caused by human-made changes in the environment is low when compared with other major causes of illness. Researchers who deal with the statistics of illness and disease, known as epidemiologists, suggest that the risk caused by any specific kind of pollution is low compared with many other risks we come in contact with every day.

For example, in the 1950s manufacturing companies routinely dumped all sorts of chemicals and other materials on pieces of land they owned around their plants. Many of these companies then later donated soil from that land, or "fill," to towns that needed to create level space for public parks and other uses. Much of that fill was heavily polluted.

One such company was Raybestos Manhattan Inc., later called Raymark, which manufactured asbestos brake shoes for automobiles. After the company closed its Stratford, Connecticut, plant in 1989, testing by the

Toxic waste stored on lands owned by industry can threaten the health of an entire community. In some cases, contaminated land has been used to create new public spaces such as parks, and has caused large-scale health problems.

federal Environmental Protection Agency showed that the plant site was contaminated not only with asbestos—a mineral fiber long linked with lung cancer—but also with chemical compounds called polychlorinated biphenyls (PCBs). PCBs have been linked to cancer in laboratory animals. Also found were high levels of lead, which have long been known to cause brain damage and retardation in children. These toxins were discovered in the parks where waste sludge from Raybestos was used as fill.

During the weeks after the discovery, town health officials closed the parks, federal and state officials pledged $8 million to bury the sites, and recommendations were made to test every child under the age of 14 for lead poisoning. A minor panic followed.

At town meetings, Dr. Mark Cullen, director of the occupational and environmental medicine program at Yale University School of Medicine, compared the risks for individuals who used the park with those risks most people take every day. He asked parents at the meetings, "Do your kids wear bicycle helmets? Do they wear seat belts? Are they vaccinated?" The risks involved in playing in a park built on Raybestos sludge fill, Cullen said, are far less than not wearing a helmet, not wearing a seat belt, or not being vaccinated.

The story in Stratford is not unique. Thousands of environmental hazards are discovered each year throughout North America. There are many dangers that we can do little, if anything, about. But there are things we *can* do to make our world less dangerous.

Many polluting wastes are produced by industry every day. As these wastes accumulate in the air, they can worsen certain respiratory conditions and can cause long-term damage to the atmosphere.

2

The Risks of Air Pollution

Smog Alert!

In many parts of North America, and in much of the industrialized world, air pollution is a common occurrence. Smog is the visible accumulation of pollutant gases in the atmosphere. It is formed when weather conditions cause the pollutants from industry, motor vehicles, and other sources to hover close to the ground rather than dissolve into the atmosphere.

Even when smog—which looks like a brown or yellow-green fog—is not clearly visible, the air we breathe is still often unhealthy, especially on warm and humid days when there is little air movement.

Although air pollution alone does not cause diseases, people with heart disease, asthma, and many other chronic illnesses feel worse on smoggy days.

People with asthma and other respiratory diseases need to be especially careful about how much time they spend outside and how much energy they exert during a smog alert.

Damage to the Ozone Layer

While most air pollution only makes underlying diseases worse, many scientists believe that use of the gas chlorofluorocarbon can actually lead to a number of cancers. Chlorofluorocarbons (CFCs), which for many years were used in aerosol sprays (they are now banned in the United States for that use), are still used in air conditioning and refrigeration systems as well as in dry-cleaning chemicals and a number of other products.

CFCs have been shown to damage the ozone layer, the part of the atmosphere that protects us from many of the ultraviolet sun rays that cause sunburn and sun-induced skin cancers. Scientists are searching for new alternatives to using CFCs in home and industrial air conditioners and refrigerators. The practice of venting

Overexposure to the sun is one of the leading causes of skin cancer, shown here. As the earth's ozone layer has been affected by pollutants, natural protection from the sun's harmful rays has lessened and unprotected exposure to the sun has become more dangerous.

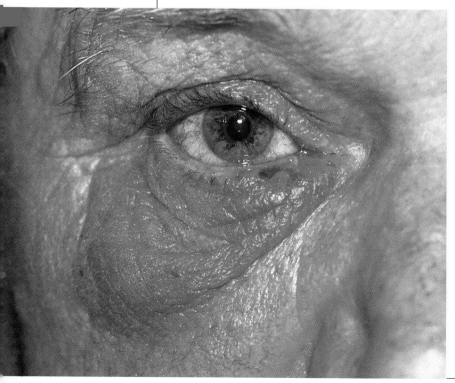

the gases from old air conditioners and refrigerators into the atmosphere when they are repaired or dismantled is no longer allowed in this country. Today, the gases must be drained into sealed containers and then recycled or chemically broken down to be made harmless.

Second-Hand Smoke

Over the years, research has increasingly shown that second-hand cigarette smoke—which is commonly called passive smoke or environmental tobacco smoke—is indeed harmful. While early efforts to limit or ban smoking in public places stressed the annoyance of cigarette smoke to nonsmokers, an ever-growing body of research has pointed to the dangers of passive smoke.

Second-hand smoke contains over 4,000 chemicals, at least 40 of which can cause cancer. Scientists believe that more than 3,000 people in the United States die every year from lung cancer caused by passive smoke.

Studies also show that children raised in homes with an adult or teenage smoker show higher rates of acute respiratory illnesses (colds, pneumonia, and ear infections) and chronic respiratory disease (asthma) than children raised in nonsmoking homes. Researchers reported in the *New England Journal of Medicine* in June 1993 that children with asthma who live with a smoker have more episodes of wheezing and worse lung function than children with asthma who live in smoke-free homes.

Research in 1993 also showed that waiters, bartenders, and other service personnel who work in businesses

where second-hand smoke is common have high rates of respiratory illness.

Indeed, epidemiologists have begun to document exactly how many cases of lung cancer in nonsmokers can be attributed to people living and working in places with a lot of second-hand smoke. A 1992 study by the Environmental Protection Agency linked second-hand smoke to as many as 300,000 lower respiratory tract infections (pneumonia and bronchitis) per year in infants and toddlers.

Since the mid-1980s, antismoking activists have been aggressive about defending the rights of nonsmokers. Today, in the United States, smoking is severely limited in public places.

Diseases Caused by "Naturally Occurring" Air Pollution

For years, miners have been among the Americans most susceptible to disease and death from pollution. Many of the earth's natural, or organic, materials that have been mined cause dust particles that, when inhaled, create chronic respiratory disease.

Perhaps the most well-known disease related to mining is "black lung" (coal worker's pneumoconiosis). This disease is common among coal miners in the eastern United States who work in deep-pit mines digging soft anthracite coal. Coal dust settles in the lung tissues and causes the lungs to become progressively more fibrous, stiff, and less able to expand and process oxygen. Symptoms usually don't appear until after more than 10 years of exposure. The condition becomes far worse in people who smoke cigarettes.

Mining, cutting, and quarrying of hard stone (especially granite), blasting, and road construction work also

put workers at risk of silicosis—a disease caused by the inhalation of particles of free silica (crystalline quartz). Symptoms of silicosis are similar to those of black lung.

Before miners' unions fought for precautions, and federal regulations for ventilation and the wearing of respirators were enacted, the majority of coal miners in the eastern United States suffered from some degree of black lung. Many died in their 30s and 40s after more than 20 years of digging in the mines. Today, the situation has been greatly improved.

Compensation for the widows and children of miners who died of black lung became a federal concern in the 1960s and

1970s. Most miners died in poverty, lacking health insurance or pensions from their employers.

Compensation for another group of miners—those who dug uranium for the United States nuclear weapons program—did not come until 1990 with the passage of the Radiation Exposure Compensation Act. This law provided payments to the families of those killed or injured in all phases of nuclear development and testing.

Asbestos: A Generation at Risk

While miners of many materials are at risk for respiratory disease, perhaps no natural material put more people at risk than asbestos. Until 1975, when it was replaced by fiberglass and other products, asbestos was the primary material that was used in insulation and fire-resistant products.

Asbestos is a mineral fiber that was used in such diverse products as pipe insulation, shingles for roofs, auto brake shoes, fire-resistant clothing, and fire-smothering blankets. A fine spray of asbestos was even applied to steel girders for bridges and buildings as a light and inexpensive fire-resistant coating.

But asbestos proved to be one of the most widespread causes of chronic respiratory disease. The tiny fibers settle in the lungs and are impossible to expel. Asbestos exposure can lead to asbestosis, a condition where the lungs become fibrous and unable to function properly (similar to black lung disease). High levels of asbestos can also cause mesothelioma—a cancer of the lung lining or the abdomen—or lung cancer.

The Risks of Air Pollution

The Radiation Exposure Compensation Act

In August 1978, Stewart Udall, an Arizona lawyer, went to Alamo, Nevada at the urging of a cousin. There, he heard the stories of families whose loved ones had been exposed to massive doses of radiation and radioactive dust during nuclear weapons testing in the 1950s.

For the next 12 years, Udall, a former congressman and secretary of the interior in the Kennedy and Johnson administrations, researched one of America's great tragedies. In the name of national security, the U.S. government had failed to acknowledge any of the dangers of mining and manufacture related to nuclear bombs, or the routine testing of those bombs.

Udall filed three lawsuits against the federal government.

One was filed on behalf of thousands of men, women, and children who claimed they were harmed by the radioactive fallout from the above-ground testing of nuclear weapons in the desert Southwest during the 1950s and early 1960s. A second lawsuit was filed on behalf of the families of Navaho Indian men who mined uranium for bomb manufacture, and were killed or disabled by cancer caused by radiation in the mines. The courts dismissed both of those lawsuits because the Federal Tort Claims Act of 1946 said the U.S. government could not be sued for damages caused by lawful federal programs.

A third lawsuit was brought by workers at the Nevada Test Site who were disabled. This lawsuit was still pending in 1993.

A Geiger counter is used to measure the amount of radiation present in a given location.

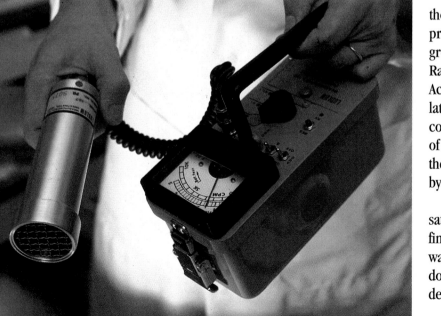

While the courts refused to allow those hurt by the nuclear weapons program to collect damages, Congress, with Udall's help, wrote the Radiation Exposure Compensation Act, passed in 1990. With this legislation, a claims board was set up to compensate workers and residents of the desert Southwest who can show they, or their dead relatives, were hurt by the nuclear weapons program.

The Radiation Exposure Compensation Act is a means of providing financial compensation. It is also a way of apologizing for the damages done and the years of secrecy and denial surrounding this issue.

During the height of asbestos usage, from the 1920s to the 1970s, an entire generation of Americans was put at risk. Workers in mining, milling, and the manufacture of asbestos products were most acutely at risk. But anyone who worked with asbestos—pipe fitters, boiler-makers, ship builders, and construction workers—were exposed to asbestos in doses high enough to cause chronic illness. And so were their families, because the workers brought asbestos fibers into their homes on the soles of their shoes and on their clothes. It is estimated that 9 million American workers, including all of those who built the huge naval fleets for World War II, had occupational exposure to asbestos.

It usually takes five years or more of regular contact with asbestos for enough fibers to accumulate in the lungs to cause disease, especially asbestosis. But less contact over a shorter time can also possibly cause disease. The first symptom of asbestosis is usually short-ness of breath when working or exercising. At this stage, a chest x-ray will show opaque patches on the lung surface. This disease is progressive, destroying lung tissue over time, and is made worse by cigarette smoking. There is no specific treatment for asbestosis, other than removing the source of exposure.

After the dangers of asbestos were finally acknowl-edged and new materials were put into use, the federal government and state governments began ordering re-moval of asbestos from all public buildings. Some states ordered removal of asbestos from homes before a sale could be finalized.

Because it is a hazardous substance, asbestos must be removed by professionals. There are also strict laws that regulate how asbestos is disposed of.

Asbestos is usually discovered through building maintenance work, since it was routinely used as pipe insulation and above ceilings for fire resistance. When this asbestos is disturbed, fibers flake off and remain in the air for weeks, exposing residents. While few, if any, people exposed in such a way would contract asbestos-related disease, doctors still do not know exactly what level of exposure is "safe." Regulations require buildings to be closed, or the areas containing asbestos to be sealed off, until the material can be removed.

In the summer of 1993, the New York City Public School system was shocked by the results of a study. It found that a number of school buildings reported to be asbestos-free in mid-1980 inspections were actually full of asbestos. Because of the massive clean-up work required, some schools did not open on schedule in the fall.

Other Indoor Hazards

A number of products that are commonly used indoors can have harmful effects on human health. In most cases, long-term problems will arise only after repeated and significant exposure to these materials. Still, the possible dangers of these chemicals and materials should always be considered. Unvented kerosene heaters, for example, can emit dangerous levels of carbon monoxide and nitrogen dioxide. Paints, certain aerosol sprays, or household pesticides can also cause severe reactions in some people if there is a lack of ventilation and fumes accumulate.

SOURCES AND POSSIBLE EFFECTS OF MAJOR INDOOR AIR POLLUTANTS

Until recently, air pollution was thought of as something that occurred outside the house and that was present in the house only when it drifted in through open windows. Today, with better sealed houses, it has become clear that the house itself, chemicals or activities within it, and even the ground the house is built upon, may contribute to air pollution indoors. Some of the pollutants found indoors are more dangerous to people than outdoor air pollution. The following is a list of chemicals and materials that may be present in a home or office building. In some cases, these elements may cause harmful effects in humans with repeated exposure. Always read manufacturers' instructions carefully before using any potentially harmful pollutants.

Pollutant	Sources	Possible Effects
Asbestos	Old or damaged insulation, fireproofing, and acoustical tiles.	Chest and abdominal cancers and lung diseases.
Carbon Monoxide	Unvented kerosene and gas heaters, leaking chimneys and furnaces, wood stoves and fireplaces, gas stoves, and tobacco smoke.	Low levels: fatigue and chest pain. High levels: impaired vision and coordination, headaches, dizziness, confusion, and nausea. Can be fatal.
Formaldehyde	Plywood, wall paneling, particleboard, fiberboard, foam insulation, fire and tobacco smoke, textiles, and glues.	Eye, nose, and throat irritation; wheezing and coughing; fatigue; skin rash; and severe allergic reactions.
Lead	Automobile exhaust, and sanding, burning, or eating of lead paint.	Impaired mental and physical development in fetuses and children, decreased coordination and mental abilities, and kidney damage.
Mercury	Some latex paints.	Vapors can cause kidney damage, long-term exposure can cause brain damage.
Nitrogen Dioxide	Kerosene heaters, unvented gas stoves and heaters, and tobacco smoke.	Eye, nose, and throat irritation; impaired lung function; and respiratory infections.
Organic Gases	Paints, paint strippers, aerosol sprays, cleansers and disinfectants, moth repellents, and air fresheners.	Eye, nose, and throat irritation; headaches; loss of coordination; nausea; and damage to liver, kidney, and nervous system.
Pesticides	Products used to kill household pests and products used on lawns or gardens.	Irritation to eyes, nose, and throat; damage to nervous system and kidneys; and cancer.
Radon	Earth and rock beneath homes, well water, and building materials.	No immediate symptoms. Estimated to cause about 10% of lung cancer deaths. Smokers are at higher risk.
Tobacco smoke	Cigarette, pipe, and cigar smoking.	Eye, nose, and throat irritation; headaches; bronchitis; pneumonia; respiratory and ear infections in children; lung cancer; and contributes to heart disease.

Source: U.S. Environmental Protection Agency, adapted from *The Inside Story: A Guide to Indoor Air Quality* (1988).

Pesticides and other chemicals are widely used in agriculture. In some cases, these products can threaten the health of both humans and other animal life in the environment.

Diseases Caused by Water or Soil Pollution

3

All food and water is threatened by pollutants from contaminated water and soil. And many of these different pollutants can make people quite sick. The wide variety of sources of water and soil pollution make the problem impossible to completely eliminate.

Agricultural Chemicals
Industrial agriculture techniques use chemical fertilizers to enhance plant growth, pesticides to kill insects that destroy food, and herbicides to clear land or keep weeds from growing. These chemicals can all cause illness if consumed in large quantities.

In health studies, large quantities of fertilizers given to laboratory animals over a short period of time have made them sick. Although the amount of these various chemicals in a person's daily food intake may not be large, scientists are not sure what the long-term effects are. Some chemicals, like the pesticide DDT, have been banned because of laboratory evidence linking them to cancer and other diseases. Others, like the herbicide Agent Orange, used by the American military during the Vietnam War, continue to be researched.

The federal and state governments regulate chemicals used in agriculture. The federal Food and Drug Administration and the Environmental Protection Agency must approve all chemicals used in agriculture. Still, more and more people are choosing to buy only chemical-free agricultural products, grown using organic fertilizers (animal manure) and natural pesticides.

Once chemicals, fertilizers, pesticides, and herbicides are used, they enter our foods in a number of ways. One point of entry is directly through the agricultural products—such as fruits and vegetables—they are used to protect. In addition, rain causes some of these chemicals to "run off" into ponds and streams that provide drinking water. Eventually, these pollutants run into the ocean, where they are a main component of pollution in salt marshes and estuaries (waterways in which a major body of water, such as an ocean, or a sea, meets a river).

High Bacteria Counts
Despite modern sanitation and water purification techniques, illnesses can still be caused by high bacteria counts either in drinking water or in fish and shellfish taken from polluted areas.

Agent Orange

Between 1962 and 1971, U.S. military forces sprayed 19 million gallons of herbicides over the jungles of South Vietnam. They sprayed in an effort to defoliate the forest areas that might serve as hiding places for enemy soldiers and guerilla fighters. Herbicides are absorbed by the soil and seep into ground water. Beginning in the mid-1970s, American veterans of the Vietnam War began experiencing a number of illnesses in larger numbers than would be expected in a normal population.

Over the past two decades, many agencies have looked into this problem. The Department of Veterans Affairs, medical groups including the National Institute of Medicine, and companies that manufacture chemical herbicides, have been engaged in research, lawsuits, and the development of new policies concerning who is responsible for the veterans' medical conditions and who should compensate the veterans.

In 1984, a lawsuit against seven companies was settled when the companies agreed to put $180 million into a fund to compensate victims of Agent Orange and their surviving family members.

The disease-causing agent in Agent Orange is believed to be dioxin, a highly toxic chemical. Doctors and scientists say that Vietnam veterans had a lower exposure to Agent Orange than civilian users of herbicides—mostly farmers—and factory workers who manufactured the product. Although no definite cause-and-effect relationship between dioxin and any of the conditions Vietnam veterans are compensated for has been proven, epidemiologists believe there is a link.

The Department of Veterans Affairs currently compensates victims or their families who suffer from any one of five diseases. (Two of the diseases were just added in June of 1993.) They are:

• Soft-tissue carcinoma, a rare cancer that affects tissues such as muscles and internal connective tissue at a wide variety of sites.

• Non-Hodgkin's Lymphoma, which forms in the lymph nodes, bone marrow, spleen, or liver. Only half of those who develop the disease live more than five years after their diagnosis.

• Hodgkin's Disease, another cancer primarily of the lymph system, which responds well to treatment. Most people who develop it survive many years.

• Chloracne, a severe skin disease similar to teenage acne but caused by chemicals. The rash and cysts normally go away or at least fade when the exposure ends.

• Porphyria Cutanea Tarda, a rare metabolic disorder that often leads to thinning or blistering skin where skin is exposed to the sun, excess pigment in skin that causes dark patches, and excess hair growth.

Dioxin has also contaminated the drinking water of a number of communities around manufacturing sites.

The most common bacteria that causes outbreaks of illness is called *Escherichia-coli,* or E-coli. E-coli are normal inhabitants of the human intestine but can increase in number and cause infection under certain circumstances. E-coli are also found in human and animal feces and when that feces contaminates water supplies an outbreak of illness can occur.

Much of the industrial world has community-wide sewage treatment. These treatment facilities take both household and industrial wastewater, filter it, and treat it with various chemicals. Waste solids are allowed to settle out into sludge, and the treated water is then released into rivers or the ocean.

Many of these systems—especially older systems serving large coastal cities such as New York, Baltimore, and San Francisco—also handle rainwater from storm drains in the streets. This water is processed with wastewater at sewage treatment plants. During heavy storms these systems can be overloaded. Storm water and wastewater, containing high levels of bacteria, can bypass treatment and flow untreated into coastal waters.

Especially in warmer weather, immediately after heavy storms, beaches are often closed to swimming. Shellfishing is also commonly restricted in areas close to sewage treatment facilities after storms. Monitoring of swimming and shellfishing areas usually alerts state and federal officials to close areas before people become sick.

Finding E-coli in drinking water is uncommon, but does occur. Although most strains of E-coli are not terribly harmful and cause only minor diarrhea, the

Although most water sources in North America are generally safe, contamination of the public water supply can cause widespread illness. In many cases, bacteria from human or animal wastes seeps into the water supply due to faulty filtration systems, severe storms, or other system breakdowns.

Diseases
Caused by
Water or Soil
Pollution

presence of any E-coli in the water supply tells authorities there are also other dangerous bacteria present.

The city of Milwaukee, Wisconsin suffered from a water contamination problem in April 1993 that made 370,000 people ill. In the history of the United States, there has never been a larger reported outbreak of disease carried by water. City officials first suspected trouble when record numbers of people needed medication for stomach-related illnesses. Tests were ordered and the results showed that Milwaukee's water contained a waterborne disease called cryptosporidiosis. This disease results in flulike symptoms in healthy people, but is deadly to those with weakened immune systems, such as AIDS patients or certain cancer patients.

Almost immediately, people were advised to boil their water before using it. Of the city's two water treatment plants, one was thought to be contaminated and was shut down.

The closed plant was cleaned and inspected. Investigators believe the cryptosporidiosis may have developed for a variety of reasons. Waste from nearby slaughterhouses, a change in the chemical treatment of the water, and a flaw in the building plan of the closed plant—the placement of a waterpipe two miles from a sewage treatment plant—were at the top of the list. Also, there had never been a test for cryptosporidiosis in the water treatment plant. Some problems were fixed right away, while others are part of a long-term plan. Just one week after the contamination was discovered, it was once again safe to drink the tap water in Milwaukee.

Lead Poisoning

For decades, lead was used in plumbing pipes, printing materials, and housepaint. Americans breathed lead fumes and inhaled lead-tainted dust from old, flaking paint. People who worked in industries such as plumbing and printing had high lead exposure.

Many older houses in North America were painted with materials containing lead. As lead paint peels and chips, it becomes a potential health hazard, especially to children.

Today, we know that lead is poisonous. It accumulates in the blood, bone marrow, and kidneys. Outward symptoms of lead poisoning—sluggishness, weight loss, and irritability—may not occur until the level of lead in the blood is extremely high. But recent research has shown that a lead level as low as 10 micrograms (a microgram is 1/100 of one gram) per deciliter of blood (a deciliter is 1/10 of a liter; one liter is a little less than one quart) can lead to a decline in intelligence on standardized tests and tests of intellectual development.

Some recent research is promising. It shows that in a group of children with moderate lead poisoning—anywhere from 25-50 micrograms per deciliter—learning development and performance on standardized tests improved significantly six months after treatment for lead poisoning. They also improved after the children's homes and schools had been cleaned of lead hazards.

Most young children are exposed to lead by drinking water that runs through lead pipes or pipes soldered with lead, or eating chips and flecks of lead paint from walls. Children in urban and industrial areas can be exposed to lead that settles in the soil from the polluted air in their neighborhoods.

Today, the American Academy of Pediatrics has guidelines for testing children for lead exposure. Most states also have programs for testing children who live in older homes, and are especially at risk. Landlords must remove lead paint, which may still be present despite the fact that lead was eliminated from paint in the late 1960s.

Houses built before the late 1960s should be tested for lead paint and lead pipes, which dent easily when tapped with a hammer. Even if the pipes do not contain lead, the main water line from a city water system may be contaminated, and faucets should be run for at least 30 seconds before pouring water to drink.

Industrial Pollution

In addition to agricultural runoff, the land and fresh water can be contaminated by industrial pollution. Factory waste is often dumped directly into rivers and streams. Some waste is buried in landfills where it can then seep into the soil and water. Other waste is left on the ground or in above-ground containers that deteriorate over time and leak into the soil.

Polychlorinated biphenyls (PCBs) are used in electrical insulation. PCBs can now be found in many harbors

Some water pollution and contamination is caused by industrial wastes. In certain cases, these wastes have been illegally dumped into waters that are intended for human consumption or other use.

Pollutants can seep into a food chain and threaten the health of all living things that are part of that chain. High levels of PCBs, for example, have been found in fish that live and breed near harbors or rivers into which certain factory wastes are dumped.

and rivers. They have been shown to cause cancer. The federal government has for years refused to issue permits to dredge harbors for fear of stirring up PCBs in the dredged material. The dredged material would then become a problem of contamination above ground.

PCBs sit on the river or ocean bottom and are eaten by animals that feed on the bottom grasses. These creatures are in turn eaten by larger fish. The pollutants are stored in the fat cells of the fish, making them potentially dangerous to eat. PCBs in particular have severely hurt the commercial fishing industry in East Coast and West Coast areas where heavy industry released PCBs into rivers and coastal waters.

Enjoying the outdoors is one of life's great pleasures. But the natural environment can pose certain threats to those who are unaware of its dangers.

4

Diseases Caused by the Natural Environment

A simple day out at the beach or the lake or hiking in the hills is full of possible health risks. Some of these risks are immediate and others are long-term. However, by learning which activities are appropriate in different environments, it is possible to reduce many of these dangers.

Altitude Sickness (Mountain Sickness)

At higher altitudes—in mountains or in cities high above sea level—the air becomes "thinner," or has less oxygen. Because of this, the heart and lungs must work harder to get oxygen to the body.

Higher than 5,000 feet above sea level—about the altitude of Denver, Colorado—people who suffer with certain respiratory problems such as asthma or other pulmonary diseases will often feel real distress. This will happen to healthy people at about 10,000 feet. At 20,000 feet, health begins to significantly deteriorate over time, even for seasoned mountain climbers.

Symptoms of altitude sickness include headache, dizziness, nausea, and even impaired mental functioning. Fluid can build up in the lungs (called pulmonary edema), leading to breathing difficulties.

For people climbing mountains, it is recommended that after ascending to about 8,000 feet, there should be a day of rest to become used to the altitude. Each day's further ascent should be limited to about 2,000 feet at a time, with another day of rest after each day of ascent.

Airplanes that travel above a few thousand feet routinely have pressurized cabins, so passengers can avoid altitude sickness. However, in a cost-cutting effort beginning in 1992, a number of airlines recycled a percentage of the cabin air and reduced the amount of pure oxygen that was put into the air supply. Flyers noticed the difference, and many complained of altitude sickness, mostly headaches and mild nausea.

Diseases Caused by Plants
"Leaves of three, let them be."

The three-leafed plants of poison ivy and poison oak are probably the most common cause of contact dermatitis, which simply means a skin rash caused by coming in contact with a particular material. A number of household plants, metals, chemicals, or certain drugs can also cause such rashes.

Poison ivy can cause a painful, itchy rash on the skin of those who come into direct contact with its leaves.

Perhaps 80 percent of all Americans have some degree of sensitivity to the substance urushiol, the oily resin found in the large and shiny leaves of poison ivy, oak, and sumac.

Even a slight exposure to the urushiol resin—coming in contact with the leaves or vines of the plant, or with something that has come in contact with the resin, such as dog fur, clothing, or garden equipment—can lead to a reaction. In fact, the amount of urushiol that could fit on a pinhead is enough to cause a reaction in the thousands of people who are extremely sensitive to it. Prompt washing with soap can lessen the reaction or stop it altogether.

The rash, also known as *Rhus dermatitis*, usually appears within a couple of days and is often gone within a week to 10 days. It does not spread by scratching, or when it is "weeping" (oozing liquid from the blisters). You must come in direct contact with the resin to spread the rash.

Contact dermatitis is annoying and may even be painful. It is usually treated with creams or ointments to relieve the itch, and steroid creams to heal the skin inflammation. In severe cases, or cases involving the eyes or the genital area, a doctor may prescribe an oral steroid drug.

Most people do not have to come in direct contact with plants to suffer discomfort. Plant allergies are among common examples of this. Depending on what plants people are sensitive to, allergies may be more severe in the spring when many plants are blooming, or later in the summer when hearty wild plants grow large and hot dry weather spreads their pollen.

Many people call allergies to pollen "hay fever," although there is no fever and hay is not the offending plant. The medical term is "seasonal allergic rhinitis." Pollen allergies cause the membranes in the nasal passages to swell, stuffing the nose. Sufferers may have clogged ears and watery eyes as well. The symptoms usually come and go as the pollen count increases and decreases.

Diseases Caused by Insects

Insect bites and stings are one of the most common warm-weather ailments. For many people, they are relatively harmless annoyances. But some individuals are especially sensitive to bites and stings of particular insects. And certain insects that carry bacteria or harmful organisms can infect people through their bites with uncomfortable diseases.

Hymenoptera Bites

Perhaps as many as 1 in 10 people are highly allergic to the venom in the stings of insects in the hymenoptera family: bees, wasps, hornets, fire ants, and yellow jackets.

These people can have an anaphylactic reaction, a life-threatening allergic reaction that calls for emergency medical treatment. Swelling may occur almost immediately around the eyes, lips, tongue, and throat. The person may have trouble breathing, which may also be accompanied by wheezing. Nausea, mental confusion, un-consciousness, and even death may occur.

For most of us, in-sect bites and stings can be treated by carefully removing the stinger, and using a cold wet cloth to reduce discom-fort. A paste of sodium bicarbonate (baking soda) and water may be applied to the sting to neutralize any acid that may be causing pain.

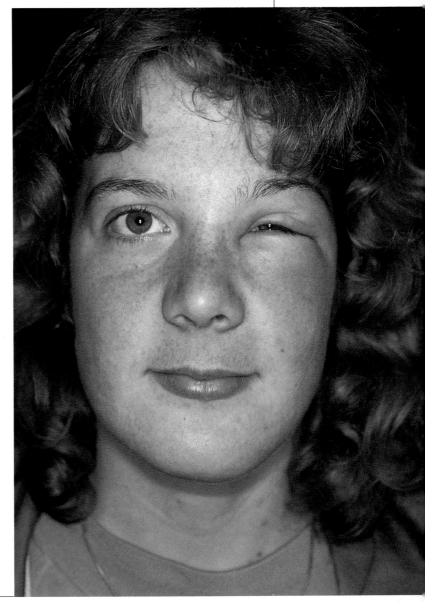

A young girl's eye swells after a bee sting. A large number of people are highly allergic to the stings or bites of certain insects.

Lyme Disease

While most insect bites are not dangerous, tick bites need special attention whenever they occur.

The deer tick, *ixodes dammini,* carries a bacteria in the spirocheete family known as *Borrelia burgdorferi,* the cause of Lyme Disease. This tick and its relatives can be found in almost every part of the United States, but it is most common along the East and West Coasts and the upper Great Lakes area of Wisconsin and Michigan. The disease was named for the site of the first identified outbreak, which occurred around the coastal Connecticut community of Lyme in the early 1980s.

Lyme Disease is often difficult to diagnose, since its initial flulike symptoms of fever, headache, and body aches are also seen in many other illnesses. But it does cause a characteristic red rash that appears within 3 to 32 days at the site of the tick bite.

A deer tick, which carries the bacteria that causes Lyme Disease.

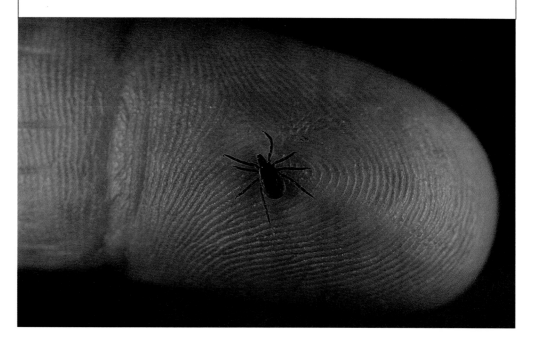

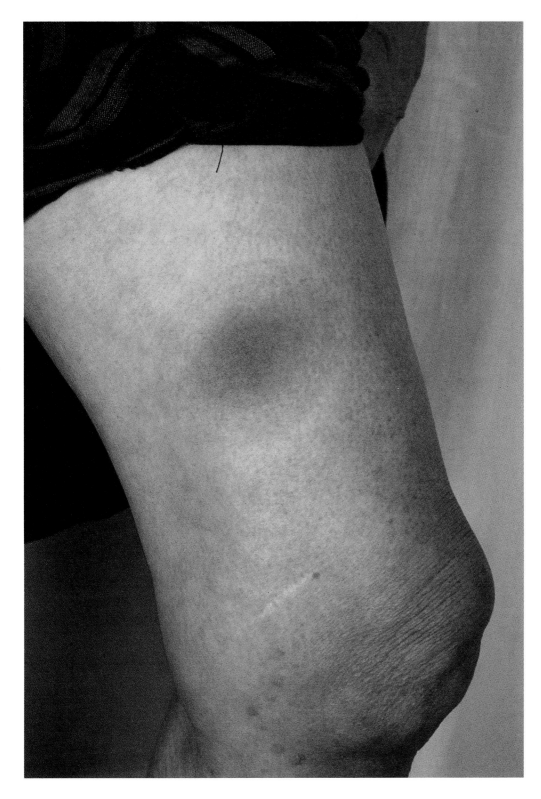

A large, red rash with a "bullseye" center is a common symptom of a deer tick bite that has caused Lyme disease.

Research has shown that infected ticks usually have to be embedded in the skin for 24 to 72 hours to cause illness. A thorough daily check for young people and adults who are outside between May and October—looking especially in warm places such as armpits, naval, genital area, anus, and behind the ears—is essential. Pets should be checked for ticks that they may have picked up outdoors. If a tick is found it should be removed. If the tick is infected, treatment for the disease should be started.

Antibiotic treatment usually cures the disease when it is caught early. In an undetected case, long-term complications can involve the joints, heart, and brain.

Rocky Mountain Spotted Fever

Wood ticks in the western United States, dog ticks in the eastern United States, and a variety of other ticks in the southern United States, can carry the organism *Rickettsia rickettsii*, which causes Rocky Mountain spotted fever.

One to eight days after being bitten by an infected tick, a person will develop headache, fever, chills, tenderness and soreness in bones and muscles, nausea, vomiting and abdominal pain. One to five days after the onset of fever, a rash will appear, beginning on the wrists and ankles and spreading to the entire body, including the scalp, palms of the hands, and soles of the feet. Infected ticks can transmit the disease in just a few hours.

Rocky Mountain spotted fever can be cured with antibiotics. Some cases can become complicated, involving the heart, lungs, and central nervous system.

Animal Bites and Rabies

Pets are responsible for the majority of animal bites. Domestic animals can carry rabies if they have been infected by a wild animal that has the rabies virus. Saliva from the bite of an infected animal causes rabies in humans.

The rabies virus affects the brain. Symptoms usually appear between three and seven weeks after a bite, and untreated rabies always leads to death. The first clear

Rabies is often transmitted through the bite of a rabid animal. Racoons are one of the most common carriers of rabies.

symptoms are pain and tingling in the area of the bite, followed by general skin sensitivity, excessive salivating, and choking when attempting to swallow liquids (known historically as hydrophobia). As the brain infection becomes severe, alternative periods of rage and calm occur, usually leading to convulsions and death. Death normally occurs within four weeks of the beginning of symptoms.

Any animal bite should be immediately washed with soap and water, and again with an antiseptic. A domestic animal that has been bitten should be confined and observed for 7 to 10 days to see if it develops the signs of rabies. It may appear nervous or vicious. Rabid wild animals become unafraid of people. If a wild animal is rabid, it should be killed immediately in a way that does not crush the brain so that the brain can be examined later. The health department should be called and the dead animal should be tested for rabies.

Many people are exposed to rabies when they check on their pet after it has had a fight with a rabid animal. The rabies virus is alive in the infected animal's saliva that may be on the fur of the pet and can enter a person's body through cuts and scrapes. It is important to wear rubber gloves when checking a pet after it has been in a fight. It is also important to make sure that pets have regular rabies vaccinations.

A doctor should be consulted for any animal bite, and he or she will need to decide if treatment for rabies is appropriate. Treatment consists of a series of five injections given over four weeks.

An 11-Year-Old Dies from Rabies

On July 5, 1993, Kelly Anne Ahrendt, 11, of Bloomingburg, New York, complained to her parents of pain in the knuckles of her left hand and numbness in her left arm. Nine days later, she died of rabies. She was the first person to die from rabies in New York State in nearly 40 years.

Since the 1970s, an epidemic of rabies has been slowly making its way north from the mid-Atlantic states into the Northeast. By 1993, rabid wild animals were routinely being destroyed in suburban and rural Connecticut, Massachusetts, and New York, and in all five boroughs of New York City. New York state authorities confirmed 1,632 cases of rabid animals in the first six months of 1993, compared to only 54 cases in all of 1989. In 1992, 1,088 New Yorkers were treated for possible rabies infection after being bitten or scratched by an animal.

Kelly Ahrendt, and her sisters and brothers, were all aware of the dangers of rabies. They stayed away from wild animals on their 18-acre property and from those in the nearby woods.

Domestic animals on the Ahrendt property—including chickens and ducks, cats, dogs, and two horses—could not have been the source of Kelly's rabies. And she did not report being bitten or scratched to her parents.

On July 8, as the family was about to set out on a trip to upstate New York, Kelly's parents took her to the pediatrician when she continued to complain about pain in her arm. The doctor suggested that the active girl probably had a sprain, but also began treating her with antibiotics for a possible strep throat infection. The Ahrendts set out on their trip.

Three days later, her parents took Kelly to a hospital in Saratoga Springs when she continued feeling ill, then the family returned home. The next day, Kelly complained of sharp pain in her arm, became confused, and began having hallucinations. Her parents took her to Horton Memorial Hospital in Middletown, near their home. On July 13 she was transferred to the Westchester County Medical Center in Valhalla, New York, where she died later that day.

An autopsy (an examination of a person for the cause of death) showed Kelly had died from viral encephalitis, a form of inflammation of the brain. Rabies is one of a number of medical conditions that can lead to viral encephalitis. By retracing the course of her illness and through other medical tests, doctors were able to confirm that she died of rabies.

The members of Kelly's family, as well as about two dozen health care workers at the three hospitals who cared for her during her illness, were later treated for possible rabies exposure.

Natural Radiation

Each year, every individual is exposed to radiation, most of it from natural sources. Eleven percent of the average person's exposure is to radiation within his or her own body, 8 percent to radiation from rocks and soil, another 8 percent to radiation from outer space. About 18 percent of the average person's annual radiation exposure each year is from human-made sources, including medical x-rays.

The largest source of radiation exposure for most people is radon, which accounts for 55 percent of total exposure. Radon is a natural gas caused by the disintegration of radium in soil and rocks that contain granite, shale, or phosphate. The amount of radon that is naturally created is usually harmless. However, if radon accumulates in an unventilated area, it can reach levels that become dangerous.

Radon gas can enter a building in a number of ways. It can come into a building through gaps or cracks in foundation walls and floors, through pores in the concrete blocks themselves, and through wall-to-wall joints.

Since radon is a gas, it can still seep into a well-insulated building. Once inside, it may become trapped in the insulation, and enough radon may collect to reach a dangerous level. Radon is harmful because it decays into radioactive atoms that bind to dust, which can be inhaled and possibly damage lung tissue.

Radon, like all radioactivity, is measured in a unit of energy called a curie. The federal Environmental Protection Agency suggests making repairs to any home

where radon levels are four picocuries of radon per liter of air or more (a picocurie is one-trillionth of a curie).

Radon detectors can be purchased in hardware or home improvement stores. Detectors are usually left untouched in a house for a period of time, then sent back to the manufacturer, who returns the test results within two weeks. Normally a radon problem can be fixed using simple caulking materials to close cracks and reseal joints, and by covering the sump (a hole in a basement floor for drainage). Small fans can also be used to circulate outside air into the house.

Testing homes for radon levels has become a common practice. Some states require homeowners to test for radon before they can sell their homes.

Diseases Caused by the Natural Environment

Exposure to Cold

Long-term unprotected exposure to the cold can lead to hypothermia, where the body loses its ability to maintain body heat, and body temperature drops. Symptoms include shivering, cold and pale skin, and slurred speech. The individual should be brought inside, or at least shielded from the cold and wind, and insulated from the ground.

Frostbite can occur to the extremities—fingers, toes, nose, and ears—especially in very cold or windy circumstances. In frostbite, the affected area actually loses blood flow, and the skin becomes hard. A person with frostbite should get the affected area covered as quickly as possible with a warm, dry material and should not rub the area.

Extreme Heat

Prolonged exposure to sun and heat can also cause problems. Sunburn is like any other burn, except that it takes longer to develop. Redness, pain, and blisters occur 6 to 12 hours after sun exposure, and discomfort reaches its peak about 24 hours after exposure.

When the heat index—temperature plus dew point (temperature at which dew forms)—approaches 100 degrees Fahrenheit (38 degrees Celsius), people are at risk for heat stress. The elderly, small children, and those working or participating in strenuous athletics outside are vulnerable at an even lower temperature.

In heat exhaustion, the heart and vascular system fail to respond to the high outside temperature. Heat exhaustion often comes on suddenly after excessive perspiration, and leaves the individual in a state resembling shock, with faintness, rapid heartbeat, low blood pressure, cold clammy skin, and nausea.

Heat exhaustion often can be treated by bringing the person into a cooler, shady area or an air-conditioned room. Loosening or removing clothes and giving the person cool, salty water to drink slowly will often help. The individual should stop work or play for the day. If the person begins to show signs of heatstroke, professional help should be summoned.

Heatstroke occurs when the body's temperature exceeds 105 degrees Fahrenheit (40 degrees Celsius), and an individual stops perspiring. (Perspiring, or sweating, is the way the body removes excess heat.) The skin becomes hot and dry, and the heart rate and breathing may become rapid. Heatstroke is caused by dehydration—lack of water in the body. The young, the old, and those taking medication that causes loss of fluids, are especially vulnerable to heatstroke, as are those working or playing outside for long periods.

Heatstroke calls for professional attention. While waiting, a person should be taken out of the sun, into an air-conditioned place if possible, and covered with cool, wet towels or sheets.

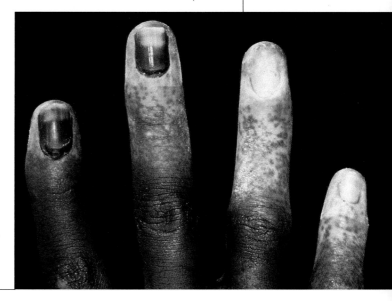

The effects of severe frostbite.

There is some speculation in the medical community that low levels of radiation emitted by microwaves, electric blankets, computers, and other appliances can pose a health threat. Some researchers believe there is a link between this radiation and cancer.

Controversies About the Environment and Your Health

With all that happens in daily life, you may be tempted to ask: How safe am I? That is a very difficult question to answer.

The natural environment poses certain dangers. And every time human actions cause a change in the environment, new dangers may be created.

But, at the same time, many government agencies and the scientific community are working to make the environment safer.

One area of controversy is the extent to which electromagnetic fields can harm us. Another subject of debate is the possibility that constant exposure to chemicals can create a vague, non-specific illness sometimes called multiple chemical sensitivity, or "Twentieth-Century Syndrome."

Whether these are real dangers or just fears, both of these conditions are caused by human-made changes to the environment. Possible solutions would drastically alter how we live.

Cancer Clusters

One of the ways health and environmental authorities were led to discover toxic waste sites was by investigating a number of mysterious "cancer clusters" (unusually high numbers of cancer patients in one geographical location), like those that occurred in Woburn, Massachusetts; Times Beach, Missouri; and Love Canal in upstate New York. Many authorities and environmental activists are asking if chemicals from toxic waste dumps may be the cause.

Although it cannot be proven that any individual's disease or death was a direct result of exposure to chemical waste, epidemiologists can make judgments that suggest causes. Each year, there are 33.2 cases of childhood leukemia per 1 million children. In a city the size of Woburn, Massachusetts, with fewer than 20,000 children, a physician might estimate that there would be only one case of leukemia a year.

But near an industrial area of Woburn, chemical companies had left thousands of drums of solvents and other chemicals out in vacant lots. Within a few years, there were dozens of cases of leukemia among children living within a few miles of the dumping site.

Such cancer clusters often occur in groups of people who work with hazardous chemicals at a particular plant. In the 1970s this happened at the Rolm and Haas chemical plant in Philadelphia. And many in the federal government presume that Vietnam veterans who have soft-tissue carcinoma, a relatively rare cancer, may have developed it because of their exposure to the herbicide Agent Orange in Vietnam.

It is difficult to prove that a person's cancer was directly caused by exposure to chemicals. But the evidence of many cancer cases in close proximity to heavy chemical use or chemical dumping has given epidemiologists information about cause and effect.

A number of government actions have been taken in the last 20 to 30 years regarding chemical pollution. The Environmental Protection Agency regulates the production, use, and disposal of chemicals that previously were unregulated. Education about the effects

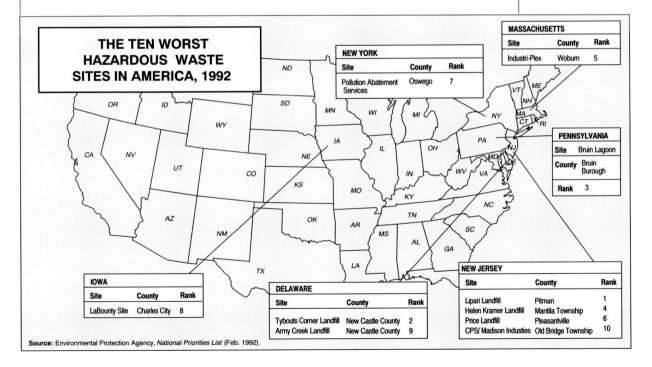

THE TEN WORST HAZARDOUS WASTE SITES IN AMERICA, 1992

MASSACHUSETTS

Site	County	Rank
Industri-Plex	Woburn	5

NEW YORK

Site	County	Rank
Pollution Abatement Services	Oswego	7

PENNSYLVANIA

Site	Bruin Lagoon
County	Bruin Burough
Rank	3

IOWA

Site	County	Rank
LaBounty Site	Charles City	8

DELAWARE

Site	County	Rank
Tybouts Corner Landfill	New Castle County	2
Army Creek Landfill	New Castle County	9

NEW JERSEY

Site	County	Rank
Lipari Landfill	Pitman	1
Helen Kramer Landfill	Mantila Township	4
Price Landfill	Pleasantville	6
CPS/ Madison Industies	Old Bridge Township	10

Source: Environmental Protection Agency, *National Priorities List* (Feb. 1992).

As we become aware of the effects of toxic wastes and other pollutants, laws are being strengthened to reduce related health risks. In many areas, the government has ordered businesses and industry to safely clean up the pollution they have caused.

of certain chemicals has led many consumers and industrial companies to use other materials. Scientists are constantly working to create products that provide benefits equal to those currently in use while creating less pollution.

Laws have begun to define who is accountable for pollution, even if it took place in the past. Guidelines are being written to describe how that pollution should be cleaned up. This after-the-fact cleanup is a slow process.

Just exactly how electricity might be responsible for cancer clusters is not clear. But some scientists believe that exposure to the oscillating impulse of high voltage power lines, or to the "jumping up" that occurs in transformers, causes damage to cells.

Although not medically proven, the electromagnetic fields and radiation from electric blankets, microwaves, and video display terminals (VDTs) have also been suggested to be the cause of both cancers and miscarriages.

Determining how to solve the potential problems with electrical and electromagnetic fields is difficult. The current solutions to these problems would be as disruptive and expensive as those to clean up chemical pollution.

Would we want to live without electricity in our homes and cities? Certainly not.

But we might work to create a new law that would increase the minimum amount of space between high-power lines and buildings. And unions representing workers who use VDTs have tried to negotiate changes in work rules that would allow women to choose not to use VDTs during their pregnancies.

Twentieth-Century Syndrome

Your symptoms are vague. You have a headache, fatigue, dizziness, anxiety, and mood swings. You have been to a dozen doctors, and no one can find out what is wrong with you. You have had a number of laboratory tests and all of the results are normal.

These are the symptoms of what some call Twentieth-Century Syndrome. To others, it is called Total-Allergy Syndrome or multiple-chemical sensitivity. Some doctors and scientists believe it is a very real condition. Others think it is the physical manifestation of clinical depression, a mental illness.

Many people who suffer from this problem believe they have found a cure when they find a "clinical ecologist." Clinical ecologists, some of whom are medical doctors, believe the disorder is caused by a breakdown of the immune system over time that leaves the sufferer "allergic" to almost all "unnatural elements," including synthetic and chemical agents. The changes suggested by clinical ecologists are difficult to accommodate, often very expensive, and rarely cure the problem.

The prescription is usually a dietary regimen of "natural" organic foods and vitamins. Some sufferers have the fillings removed from their teeth. Others stop working. Those with the worst cases often sell their homes and move to secluded places, where they live in homes containing as little synthetic material as possible.

There is an entire community in Arizona where people who suffer from multiple chemical allergies live. Some live in porcelain house trailers, wear only white cotton clothes, and "air out" their mail before bringing it into their home. They do this in order to minimize their contact with the substances to which they believe they are sensitive. While some of their physical symptoms are helped, these people are still anxious, and are often terrified of unanticipated contamination.

The American College of Physicians has declared that this syndrome does not exist, and that clinical ecology is a hoax that takes advantage of depressed, anxious people. The possibility of such a syndrome is fed by the fears that some people have about the damage caused to the environment by excessive use of chemicals. Many doctors argue that the "disease" is as much political and sociological as it is medical. It is seen more in well-educated, economically secure people than in poor or working-class groups.

A variety of health-care providers have suggested to many sufferers that they visit a psychiatrist or psychologist to get another opinion about their condition. But patients usually shun such suggestions and continue to search for a cure. So it is difficult to get any reliable research about whether these people really do show depressive illness when given objective diagnostic tests.

Because the practice of clinical ecology seems to be growing, these people have an easier time finding someone to treat them than in the past. And because most sufferers are middle-class or well off, they are usually able to pay for continued treatment, even if it is not benefiting them in any real way.

Doctors have been able to perform psychiatric tests on some people displaying the symptoms of Twentieth-Century Syndrome. For instance, a factory worker will get a referral to an occupational health specialist as part of a workman's compensation claim for unspecified symptoms that the worker believes are coming from constant exposure to chemicals in the workplace.

In these instances, researchers have found that a large number of people referred for such physical ailments have treatable symptoms of depression, anxiety, or both. Many of these people fear that their workplace exposure is causing them physical harm. When treated for their mental illness, a large percentage of these people are able to return to work without fear of their health being harmed by their working environment. Their lack of fear, in turn, will often cause the physical symptoms to disappear.

Doing your part in helping to keep the world clean is just one way you can have a real effect on your environment.

What Effect Can We Have?

If our environment were cleaner, there might not be so much fear about adverse health effects—even if the actual health effects are mostly non-life-threatening.

Individuals cannot significantly change the environment alone. But everyone can work to come to some agreement on one question: What level of environmental danger and risk should we live with in order to balance our health with societal goals and economic development? We also need to agree on what elements of environmental health and safety should be individually maintained and what elements should be regulated by state or federal government agencies.

Glossary

altitude sickness A feeling of dizziness, nausea, and difficulty breathing caused by high altitudes.

asthma A condition characterized by congestion of the bronchial tubes that causes coughing, wheezing, and difficulty breathing.

bacteria One-celled, microscopic organisms, some of which cause infection.

cancer cluster A region, city, or neighborhood where more people suffer from cancer than would normally be expected in that population.

chloracne A severe skin rash, similar to normal adolescent acne, that is caused by exposure to chemicals.

chlorofluorocarbons A group of chemicals that have been used in aerosol sprays and refrigeration. They have been shown to harm the earth's atmosphere, specifically the ozone layer.

contact dermatitis A skin rash caused by contact with a particular substance. The most common contact dermatitis is caused by poison ivy, oak, or sumac.

electromagnetic field The force field that is created by the oscillating electrical impulses around electrical wires and electrical appliances.

epidemiology The study of diseases, how they spread, and how they occur in varying populations.

frostbite A condition caused by exposure of skin to extreme cold.

heat exhaustion A sudden onset of faintness, rapid heartbeat, low blood pressure, and cold, clammy skin that is caused by long exposure to high heat and humidity.

heat stroke A condition caused by loss of body fluids. The body temperature rises to above 105 degrees Fahrenheit and the individual stops perspiring.

herbicide A chemical, or combination of chemicals used to kill plants.

Lyme disease Caused by the eastern deer tick and its relatives, Lyme disease symptoms mimic flu, except for the characteristic "bullseye" rash that develops. Early detection and treatment with antibiotics cures the disease.

mesothelioma A cancer of the lung lining or abdominal wall, mesothelioma is most common among those with long-term exposure to asbestos.

ozone layer The layer of the earth's atmosphere that is most important in blocking out the harmful ultra-violet rays that cause sunburn and skin cancers.

parasite An organism that depends on another organism for nourishment and protection, some of which cause infection.

pesticide A chemical or biological agent used to kill insects that eat vegetables and grains.

pollution The outcome of discharge of wastes into the environment.

polychlorinated biphenyl (PCB)
A chemical composition used for many years as insulation for electrical transformers. PCBs have been shown in laboratory tests to cause cancer.

rabies A virus caused by exposure to the saliva from an animal infected with rabies. The virus affects the brain and central nervous system, causing convulsions and death.

radon Naturally occuring radioactive gas caused by the breakdown of radium in soil that contains granite, shale, and phosphate.

salmonella A bacteria found in meats, poultry, eggs, and unpasteurized dairy products.

second-hand smoke The smoke a nonsmoker inhales from nearby cigarettes.

smog Visibly polluted air, smog is the reflection of light through particles of polluted gases in the atmosphere.

soft-tissue carcinoma A rare cancer that affects tissues such as muscles and internal connective tissue at a variety of sites within the body.

Twentieth-Century syndrome A condition that is characterized by fatigue, headache, dizziness, and anxiety.

typhoid fever A bacterial infection that is most common in underdeveloped countries where sanitation is bad, it is contracted through contaminated food or water. Fever and achiness are present, as are vomiting, diarrhea, and intestinal pain.

urushiol The active ingredient in poison ivy, oak, and sumac.

video display terminal (VDT) The video portion of computer, word processing, and video game systems.

wastewater Untreated or partially treated water that is released into fresh or ocean water either from an industrial plant or a sewage treatment facility.

wheezing Loud, labored breathing that is characteristic of people with conditions in which the bronchial tubes that carry oxygen to and from the lungs are constricted and/or stiff.

For Further Reading

Anderson, Modelyn K. *Environmental Diseases*. New York: Watts, 1987.

Becklake, John. *Pollution*. New York: Watts, 1990.

Edelson, Ed. *Clean Air*. New York: Chelsea House, 1992.

Hare, Tony. *Toxic Waste*. New York: Watts, 1991.

Kiefer, Irene. *Poisoned Land: The Problems of Hazardous Waste*. New York: Macmillan Children's Group, 1981.

Leggett, Dennis. *Troubled Waters*. North Bellmore, NY: Marshall Cavendish, 1991.

Peissel, Michel and Allen, Missy. *Dangerous Insects*. New York: Chelsea House, 1993.

Yount, Lisa. *Cancer*. San Diego, CA: Lucent Books, 1991.

Index

Photo Credits:

Page 4: ©Richard Hutchings/Photo Researchers, Inc.; p. 7: North Wind; p. 8: Environmental Protection Agency; p. 12: ©Jeff Greenberg/Photo Researchers, Inc.; p. 14: Environmental Protection Agency; p. 16: Science Photo Library/Photo Researchers, Inc.; p. 18: ©Richard Hutchings/Science Source/Photo Researchers, Inc.; p. 20: ©Kenneth Murray/Photo Researchers, Inc.; p. 22: ©Hank Morgan/Science Source/Photo Researchers, Inc.; p. 26: ©Blackbirch Graphics/USDA Photo; pp. 31, 60: Environmental Protection Agency; p. 33: ©Wil Wilkins Images/Photo Researchers, Inc.; p. 34: ©James Prince/Photo Researchers, Inc.; p. 35: ©Bill Bachman/Photo Researchers, Inc.; p. 36: National Park Service; p. 39: ©Michael Gadomski/Photo Researchers, Inc.; pp. 41, 42: ©Scott Camazine/Photo Researchers, Inc.; p. 43: ©Larry Mulvehill/Photo Researchers, Inc.; p. 45: ©Blackbirch Graphics; p. 49: ©Will & Deni McIntyre/Photo Researchers, Inc.; p. 51: ©by SIU/Photo Researchers, Inc.; p. 52: ©Stuart Rabinowitz; p. 56: ©Sam C. Pierson, Jr./Photo Researchers, Inc.